Introduction :

Welcome to this special Father's Day book, a heartfe
dads out there. Within these pages, you'll find a cc
and cherished memories that honor the unique bonc ... ... their
children.

This book is a celebration of fatherhood, filled with classic dad jokes that will
have you smiling and groaning, personalized jokes that reflect the individuality of
each father-child relationship, heartwarming stories that capture the essence of
unconditional love, and engaging activities that foster bonding and creativity.

We've also included trivia challenges, brain-teasing riddles, fun facts, and
reflective questions to entertain, challenge, and inspire meaningful conversations.
It's a treasure trove of joy, appreciation, and the simple pleasures that fathers
bring to our lives.

Whether you're a dad looking for a chuckle, a child wanting to express gratitude,
or someone celebrating a beloved dad, this book is a delightful companion that
captures the essence of fatherhood and the importance of the father-child bond.

So, join us on this journey of laughter and love. Flip through the pages, share the
jokes, embrace the heartwarming moments, and cherish the memories. Happy
Father's Day!

If you enjoyed this book,
we would be immensely grateful if you could take a few moments
to share your thoughts by writing **an honest review.**
Your feedback is invaluable and helps us continue creating
content that resonates with readers like you.
**Thank you for your support and for being a part of our creative
journey**.

Classic Dad Jokes

Get ready for a collection of timeless and cringe-worthy dad jokes that will have you rolling your eyes and laughing at the same time. These jokes have been passed down through generations of dads, bringing laughter and groans wherever they're shared.

Why don't skeletons fight each other?

They don't have the guts!

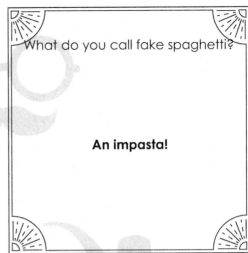

What do you call fake spaghetti?

An impasta!

How does a penguin like its steak?

Well-done!

How do you organize a space party?

You "planet"!

Why don't scientists trust atoms?

Because they make up "everything"!

I used to hate facial hair...

But then it "grew on me"!

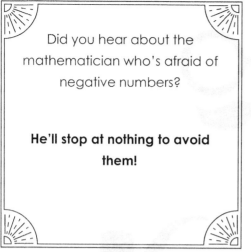

Did you hear about the mathematician who's afraid of negative numbers?

He'll stop at nothing to avoid them!

Why did the scarecrow win an award?

Because he was outstanding in his field!

Why did the scarecrow join Instagram?

Because he wanted to keep up with the corny

I have a joke about paper...

But it's tearable!

I used to play piano by ear, but now I use my...

"hands"!

How do you catch a squirrel?

Climb a tree and "act like a nut"!

I used to play piano by ear,

But now I use my hands.

Why don't eggs tell jokes?

Because they might crack up!

I'm on a seafood diet.

I see food, and I eat it!

Why did the bicycle fall over?

It was "two-tired"!

What's brown and sticky?

A "stick"!

What's orange and sounds like a parrot?

A "carrot"!

I have a joke about clouds...

But it's over your head.

I'm reading a book about anti-gravity.

It's impossible to put down!

What do you get when you cross a snowman and a vampire?

Frostbite!

What did one wall say to the other wall?

I'll meet you at the "corner"!

Did you hear about the mathematician who's afraid of...

Negative numbers? He'll "stop at nothing" to avoid them!

Why did the smartphone bring a sweater?

Because it heard it might get a little chilly on the web!

What do you call a funny video about a potato on TikTok?

A "spud-tacular" viral sensation!

Why did the stadium get hot after the game?

All of the fans left!

What do you call a bear with no teeth?

A gummy bear!

Why did the golfer bring two pairs of pants?

In case he got a "hole in one"!

I have a joke about chairs...

But it's not gonna stand up.

I told my wife she should embrace her mistakes...

She gave me a hug!

What did the grape say when it got stepped on?

Nothing, it just "let out a little wine"!

I have a joke about electricity...

But it's shocking!

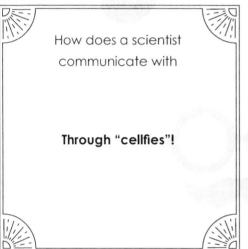

How does a scientist communicate with

Through "cellfies"!

What did one hat say to the other hat?

You stay here, I'll go on "ahead"!

What do you call a fake noodle?

An "impasta"!

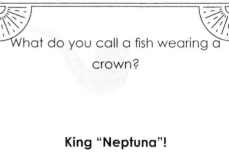

What do you call a fish wearing a crown?

King "Neptuna"!

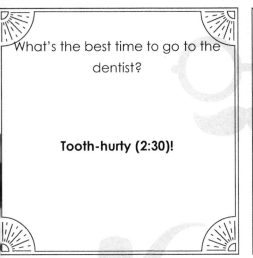

What's the best time to go to the dentist?

Tooth-hurty (2:30)!

How does a penguin build its house?

Igloos it together!

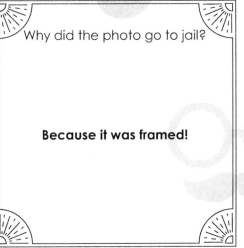

Why did the photo go to jail?

Because it was framed!

How do you make a tissue dance?

You put a little "boogie" in it!

I have a joke about chemistry...

But all the good ones Argon!

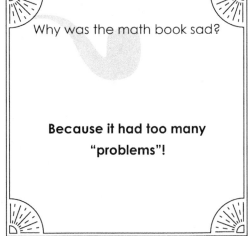

Why was the math book sad?

Because it had too many "problems"!

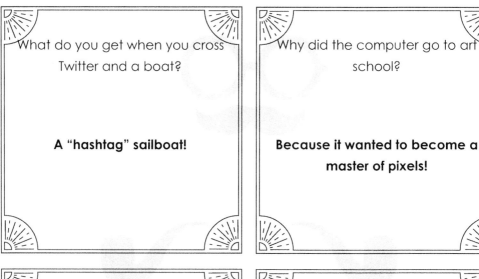

What do you get when you cross Twitter and a boat?

A "hashtag" sailboat!

Why did the computer go to art school?

Because it wanted to become a master of pixels!

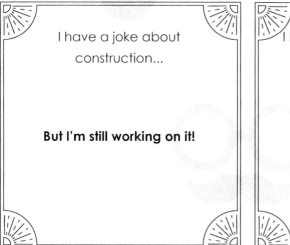

I have a joke about construction...

But I'm still working on it!

I have a joke about animals...

But it's not quite purr-fect!

What do you call a computer that sings?

A Dell!

What did the buffalo say when his son left for college?

Bison!

Did you hear about the restaurant on the moon?

Great food, but no atmosphere!

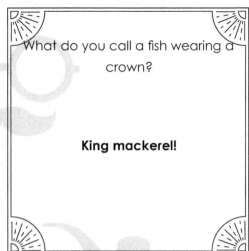

What do you call a fish wearing a crown?

King mackerel!

I have a joke about pencils...

But it's pointless.

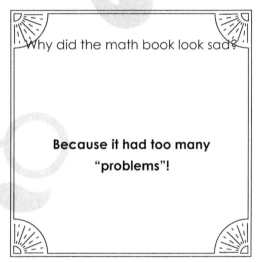

Why did the math book look sad?

Because it had too many "problems"!

I went to buy some camouflage pants, but I...

Couldn't find any!

I'm friends with 25 letters of the alphabet...

I don't know "Y"!

I have a joke about pizza...

But it's a little cheesy.

Why did the scarecrow get an Instagram account?

Because it heard there were lots of followers in the field!

I have a joke about time travel...

Never mind, you guys didn't like it.

I have a joke about gardening...

But I don't want to spoil it.

I have a joke about math...

But it's too complex!

Did you hear about the kidnapping at the playground?

It's okay, he "woke up"!

Wordplay and Puns

If you appreciate the art of wordplay and clever puns, this section is for you. Prepare to have your linguistic skills put to the test with witty riddles, playful puns, and clever twists on words. These jokes will tickle your funny bone and showcase the humorous side of language.

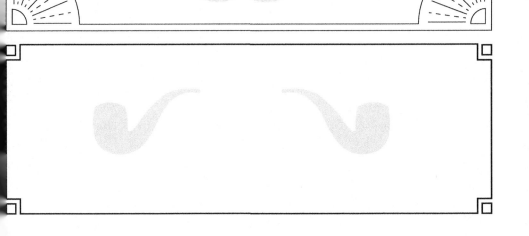

I started a band called 1023 Megabytes.

We haven't gotten a gig yet.

Why did the tomato turn red?

Because it saw the salad dressing!

Why did the math book look sad?

Because it had too many problems!

What's brown and sticky?

A stick!

I used to play piano by ear, but now I use my hands.

It's much more effective!

I went to buy some camouflage pants, but I couldn't find any.

They must have blended in with the rest of the clothes!

What did one wall say to the other wall?

I'll meet you at the corner.

I told my wife she should do lunges to stay in shape.

That would be a big step forward!

I asked the gym instructor if he could teach me to do the splits.

He replied, "How flexible are you?" I said, "I can't make it on Mondays."

How does a train eat?

It goes chew, chew!

Did you hear about the guy who invented Lifesavers?

They say he made a mint!

I'm on a seafood diet.

Every time I see food, I eat it!

Situational Jokes

Life is full of funny and relatable situations, and dads have a knack for finding humor in everyday experiences. In this section, we explore the humorous side of family life, parenting adventures, and those awkward moments we can all relate to.

Why did the father clock get in trouble?

It couldn't keep its hands off the children!

Why did the father become a landscaper?

He wanted to "mow" the lawn and make it a "cutting-edge" experience!

Why did the dad become a coach?

He wanted to "train" his kids to be the best they can be!

Why did the dad bring a whistle to the amusement park?

He wanted to be the official "fun coordinator" and make sure everyone had a blast!

Why do dads love playing board games?

They can't resist the chance to say, "I'm the dad-est player of them all!"

Why do dads love playing video games with their kids?

It gives them a chance to show off their "dad-ication" and gaming skills!

Why did the dad bring a ladder to the barbeque?

He heard the steaks were on another level!

Why do dads make terrible DJs?

They always "drop the beat" on their favorite songs!

Why did the father enroll in a cooking class?

He wanted to "whip up" some culinary skills and impress the family!

Why do dads love going to the farmer's market?

They enjoy "picking" out the best produce and cracking jokes with the vendors!

Why did the dad bring a map to the amusement park?

He didn't want to get "lost" in the fun and miss out on any attractions!

Why did the father bring a picnic blanket to the park?

He wanted to create a cozy "joke zone" and have a pun-filled picnic!

Why do dads make great detectives?

They have "dad-ar" that can spot any hidden mess!

Why did the dad wear a belt with suspenders?

He wanted to "hold up" his reputation as the ultimate dad!

Why did the dad take a ladder to the soccer game?

He heard the competition was "off the charts" and wanted to rise above it!

Why did the father bring a grill to the beach?

He wanted to have a "barbecue by the seashore" and enjoy a sizzling time!

Why do dads love going to the zoo with their kids?

They enjoy "lion" about the different animals and creating wild memories!

Why do dads love telling jokes at the family dinner table?

They enjoy "spicing" up the conversation and serving laughter as a side dish!

Why did the dad take a nap on the watchtower?

He was on "paternal" duty!

Why did the dad bring a map to the beach?

He wanted to "navigate" the waves and find the perfect spot!

Why did the father bring a broom to the family reunion?

To sweep his relatives off their feet with his dad jokes!

Why do dads always carry spare change in their pockets?

They're prepared to make their kids' day by giving them "cents" of joy!

Why did the father bring a camera to the family barbecue?

He wanted to "grill" everyone with his dad jokes and capture the laughter!

Why did the dad bring a compass to the hiking trip?

He didn't want to "lose his way" and miss out on telling jokes on the trail!

Why did the father wear sunglasses during his karate class?

Because he didn't want to "throw shade" on his opponents!

Why did the father become a chef?

He wanted to "spice up" family dinners and serve some dad-licious meals!

Why do dads always have a measuring tape in their pockets?

They're "masters" at sizing up any situation!

Why did the dad bring a telescope to the park?

He wanted to "scope out" the perfect spot for a family picnic!

Why do dads love telling jokes while driving?

It helps them "steer" the conversation in a funny direction!

Why do dads always have a joke ready when fixing something?

It helps them "hammer" home the point and make repairs more entertaining!

Why did the dad bring a bucket to the movie theater?

Just in case there were "popcorn" emergencies!

Why did the dad bring a ladder to the concert?

He wanted to get a "higher note" on the music!

Why did the dad bring a fishing rod to the party?

He wanted to "reel in" some good times and great conversations!

Why do dads love telling jokes while gardening?

It helps them "cultivate" laughter and make their plants grow happier!

Why did the dad bring a toolbox to the camping trip?

He wanted to "nail" the perfect outdoor experience and fix any mishaps!

Why did the father bring a notepad to the beach?

To "shore" up his dad jokes and jot down any waves of inspiration!

Why did the father bring a ruler to the bakery?

To measure how "sweet" the pastries were!

Why do dads love gardening?

It gives them the perfect opportunity to "dig" up some dad jokes!

Why do dads love playing hide-and-seek with their kids?

They can never resist the opportunity to say, "I'm hiding... from my chores!"

Why did the father become a referee?

He loved having the final say and blowing the whistle on dad jokes!

Why do dads make great storytellers during bedtime?

They have a knack for creating "dreamy" tales and putting kids to sleep!

Why do dads love playing catch with their kids?

They enjoy the opportunity to "catch" up on life and share moments together!

Why do dads always bring a camera to a barbecue?

They love to "grill" the guests with their dad jokes!

Why did the dad buy a boat?

He wanted to become the "captain" of his own dadventure!

Why did the father bring a camera to the park?

He wanted to capture the "picture-perfect" moments with his kids!

Why did the dad bring a toolbox to the beach?

Just in case he needed to "sand-wich" his jokes with some handy puns!

Why did the father bring a fishing net to the pool party?

He wanted to "catch" all the laughter and make a splash with his jokes!

Why did the dad bring a whistle to the family picnic?

He wanted to be the official "fun director" and keep everyone laughing!

Why did the dad become a barber?

He wanted to "cut" down on his kids' haircuts expenses!

Why do dads always carry a pencil behind their ear?

In case they need to "draw" on their dad wisdom!

Why did the dad bring a toolbox to the baseball game?

In case someone needed to be "hammered" with a dad joke!

Why do dads love going on road trips?

They enjoy "steering" the family toward adventure and telling jokes along the way!

Why do dads love going to the amusement park with their kids?

They enjoy "roller-coasting" through the ups and downs of parenthood!

Why do dads love telling jokes during car rides?

It helps them "drive" home the laughter and make the journey more enjoyable!

Why did the dad bring a toolbox to the picnic?

Just in case they needed to "nail" the perfect outdoor gathering!

Why did the father become an umpire?

He loved "calling the shots" and keeping the game in check!

Why do dads make excellent tour guides?

They're experts at "dad-venturing" and finding the best routes!

Why did the dad bring a notepad to the playground?

To jot down some "playful" ideas for fun activities with the kids!

Why did the dad bring a notepad to the soccer game?

To "goal" down his dad jokes and keep score of how many laughs he gets!

Why did the father bring a ladder to the family gathering?

He wanted to "rise above" with his dad jokes and reach new levels of humor!

Why did the dad bring a calculator to the grocery store?

He wanted to "add" up the savings and make sure he got the best deals!

Why did the father bring a flashlight to the camping trip?

He wanted to "light up" the night with his illuminating dad jokes!

Why did the dad bring a map to the road trip?

He didn't want to "drive" his family crazy and get lost along the way!

Why did the dad take up gardening?

He wanted to "grow" his dad joke repertoire and cultivate a green thumb for comedy!

Why did the dad always bring a camera to family gatherings?

Because he loved capturing "punny" moments and making memories in a snapshot!

Why do dads love playing board games with their kids?

They can't resist the chance to say, "I'm the dad-est player of them all!"

Why do dads love telling jokes while mowing the lawn?

It helps them "cut" through the boredom and make yard work more fun!

Why do dads love grilling in the backyard?

They enjoy being the "barbecue-ther" of delicious food and puns!

Why did the dad always carry a pencil behind his ear?

Because he was constantly "writing" down his dad jokes and never wanted to forget them!

Why did the dad bring a ladder to the sporting event?

He wanted to "climb" to new heights of cheering and show his support from above!

Why did the dad become a teacher?

He wanted to "educate" his students with dad jokes and be the class clown role model!

Why did the dad bring a camera to the school talent show?

He wanted to "capture" the amazing performances and create lasting memories!

Why did the dad bring a shovel to the beach?

Because he wanted to dig "deep" into some quality family time!

Why did the dad take up gardening?

Because he wanted to "grow" a special bond with his kids and watch them blossom!

Why did the dad bring a ladder to the soccer game?

Because he wanted to see his kids "rise" to the occasion and score some goals!

Why did the dad open a bakery?

Because he kneaded a way to provide for his "roll" models!

Why did the dad bring a ladder to the soccer game?

Because he wanted to cheer his kids on from a "higher" level and show his "support"!

Why did the dad start a gardening project?

Because he wanted to "plant" the seeds of knowledge and teach his kids about nature's beauty!

Why did the dad start a band with his kids?

Because he wanted to be the "dad-lead" singer and make some rockin' memories!

Why did the dad take his kids on a fishing trip?

Because he wanted to "reel" them in and catch some unforgettable memories!

Why did the dad volunteer to coach the little league?

Because he wanted to "pitch" in and help his kids develop their sports skills!

Why did the dad become a gardener?

Because he wanted to "grow" a strong bond with his children and watch them "blossom"!

Why did the dad bring a map to the amusement park?

Because he wanted to "navigate" through the rides and ensure a day of fun for his family!

Why did the dad become a referee for kids' sports?

Because he wanted to "call the shots" and show his kids the importance of fair play!

Why did the dad always carry a toolbox?

Because he was the go-to "fixer-upper" and could handle any household challenge!

Why did the dad become a taxi driver for his kids?

Because he wanted to chauffeur them around and be their "driving" force!

Why did the dad go to the bakery with his kids?

Because he wanted to "doughnut" miss out on the opportunity to bond over treats!

Why did the dad bring a camera to the school play?

Because he wanted to "capture" every moment and be the "flashiest" dad in the audience!

Why did the dad become a teacher's assistant?

Because he wanted to be involved in his kids' education and show that he's an "A+ dad"!

Why did the dad join a DIY workshop?

Because he wanted to "hammer" home the importance of learning new skills and being handy!

Why did the dad enroll in a cooking class?

Because he wanted to "spice" up family dinners with his culinary dad jokes!

Why did the dad dress up as a superhero for Halloween?

Because he wanted to be their real-life "super-dad" and save the day!

Why did the dad bring a map on the family road trip?

Because he wanted to be the "navigator-in-chief" and ensure a smooth journey!

Why did the dad take his kids fishing?

Because he wanted to "reel" in quality time with his children and make lasting memories!

Why did the dad enroll in a cooking class?

Because he wanted to "spice up" family dinners and become a master of the "dad cuisine"!

Why did the dad become a storyteller?

Because he wanted to "weave" tales of imagination and create magical memories with his kids!

Why did the dad become a referee for kids' sports?

Because he wanted to show off his "dad-lining" skills and keep the game fair and fun!

Why did the dad bring a camera to the school play?

Because he wanted to "capture" every moment and be their biggest fan!

Why did the dad take his kids to the amusement park?

Because he wanted to "ride" the roller coasters and experience thrilling adventures!

Why did the dad go to the beach with his kids?

Because he wanted to "sand" out as a fun-loving dad and make a splash with his family!

Why did the dad start a band with his kids?

Because he wanted to "harmonize" with his children and create a family "hit"!

Why did the dad learn magic tricks?

Because he wanted to "amaze" his kids and make everyday moments extraordinary!

Why did the dad take up cooking?

Because he wanted to "spice" up family meals and show off his culinary skills!

Why did the dad take up painting?

Because he wanted to "brush" up on his artistic abilities and unleash his creativity!

Why did the dad become a puzzle enthusiast?

Because he wanted to "piece" together fun-filled moments and challenge his kids' minds!

Why did the dad become a comedian?

Because he wanted to "crack" jokes and make his kids laugh until their sides hurt!

Why did the dad become a DIY enthusiast?

Because he wanted to "hammer" home the importance of resourcefulness and problem-solving skills!

Why did the dad become a coach?

Because he wanted to "play" an active role in his children's lives and help them reach their goals!

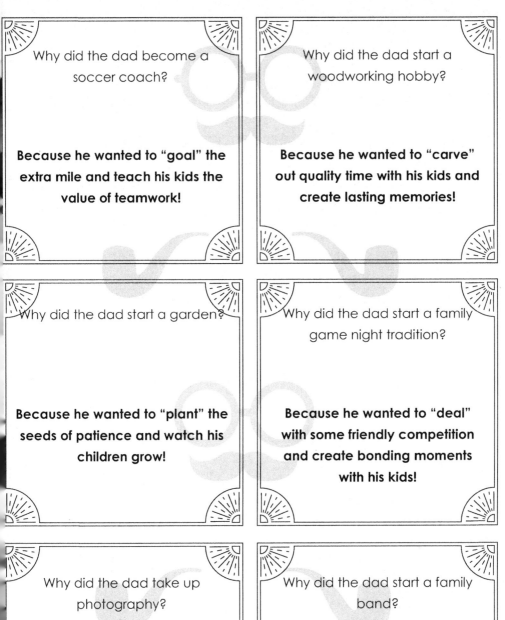

Why did the dad become a soccer coach?

Because he wanted to "goal" the extra mile and teach his kids the value of teamwork!

Why did the dad start a woodworking hobby?

Because he wanted to "carve" out quality time with his kids and create lasting memories!

Why did the dad start a garden?

Because he wanted to "plant" the seeds of patience and watch his children grow!

Why did the dad start a family game night tradition?

Because he wanted to "deal" with some friendly competition and create bonding moments with his kids!

Why did the dad take up photography?

Because he wanted to "capture" all the precious moments with his family and create lasting memories!

Why did the dad start a family band?

Because he wanted to "harmony"ze their talents and create beautiful music together!

Personalized Jokes

No one knows you better than your dad, and that means he's an expert at crafting personalized jokes just for you. In this section, we celebrate the unique bond between father and child with jokes that are tailored to your inside jokes, shared memories, and individual quirks.

Why did the dad always win at chess?

Because he's a master strategist, just like he's mastered the art of finding the TV remote!

Why did the dad love to play golf?

Because he could always score a "hole-in-dad" with his amazing swing and sense of humor on the golf course!

Why did the dad become a fishing enthusiast?

Because he knows how to "reel" in the laughter, always has a "catchy" joke, and enjoys the tranquility of fishing!

Why did the dad become a gardening expert?

Because he has a "green thumb," knows how to "dig" deep for dad jokes, and can make any plant "blossom" with laughter!

Why did the dad become a fishing expert?

Because he can "reel" in the laughs with his jokes, knows all the "fin"-tastic fishing spots, and loves to "tackle" humor!

Why did the dad become a barbecue expert?

Because he knows how to "grill" it with his jokes, has the perfect "sauce" of humor, and can "smoke" the competition!

Why did the dad become a chef?

Because no one can grill a burger or flip pancakes like he can! He's the king of the backyard barbecue!

Why did the dad become a music enthusiast?

Because he can "tune" out the world and create the perfect playlist for any occasion, rocking the dad vibes!

Why did the dad become a DIY expert?

Because he's a "hammer" of all trades, knows how to "nail" a project, and can fix anything with his dad skills!

Why did the dad become a coffee connoisseur?

Because he knows how to "espresso" his love for coffee, always has a "brew-tiful" joke, and enjoys a "latte" of humor!

Why did the dad become a music enthusiast?

Because he's always "in tune" with comedy, knows how to "harmony"ze a joke, and can "rock" the stage with his dad humor!

Why did the dad become a car enthusiast?

Because he's always "revving" up with funny one-liners, knows all the "driving" puns, and can "steer" a good laugh!

Why did the dad become a golfer?

Because he always knows how to "drive" the ball and "putt" a smile on everyone's face with his jokes!

Why did the dad become a coffee connoisseur?

Because he knows how to brew up a mean cup of coffee and always starts the day with a strong dose of humor!

Why did the dad become a tech guru?

Because he's always "plugged in" with the latest gadgets, knows how to "debug" any tech issue, and codes dad jokes!

Why did the dad become a car enthusiast?

Because he's always "driven" to tell a good joke, knows all the "rev-ved" up car trivia, and has a "wheelie" funny side!

Why did the dad become a DIY guru?

Because he's "handy" with a joke, knows how to "nail" the punchline, and can "build" a laugh from scratch!

Why did the dad become a coffee connoisseur?

Because he brews up "roast-ful" humor, knows all the "grounds" for a good joke, and can "espresso" his funny side!

Why did the dad love to watch action movies?

Because he's the real-life superhero who can fix anything around the house with just a roll of duct tape!

Why did the dad become a photography enthusiast?

Because he's a master at capturing precious family moments and knows how to "focus" on the funniest angles!

Why did the dad become a bookworm?

Because he loves getting lost in a good book, knows all the "puns" in literature, and can "novel" you with jokes!

Why did the dad become a cooking maestro?

Because he's a "culinary king," knows how to "spice up" any dish, and can turn cooking into a "recipe" for laughter!

Why did the dad become a bookworm?

Because he's "well-read" in humor, knows all the "chapter and verse" of funny stories, and can "turn the page" to laughter!

Why did the dad become a golf fanatic?

Because he knows how to "tee off" a great punchline, has a "swing" at humor, and can "putt" a smile on anyone's face!

Why did the dad love to go fishing?

Because he's a master angler who can reel in a big catch and tell "fishy" stories like no one else!

Why did the dad become a camping enthusiast?

Because he loves "pitching" a tent, telling campfire stories, and roasting marshmallows with the family!

Why did the dad become a sports fanatic?

Because he's a "cheerleader" for his favorite team, knows all the sports trivia, and has a "ball" with dad humor!

Why did the dad become a camping aficionado?

Because he knows how to "pitch" a good joke, enjoys the great outdoors, and can "roast" his way to dad humor!

Why did the dad become a movie buff?

Because he can "script" a hilarious joke, knows all the "blockbuster" films, and enjoys a "reel"-ly good punchline!

Why did the dad become a travel enthusiast?

Because he's always "jetting" off with hilarious stories, knows the best "desti-jokes," and can "travel" you with laughter!

Why did the dad always have a toolbox handy?

Because he's a DIY expert who can fix anything, from leaky faucets to broken hearts!

Why did the dad become a car enthusiast?

Because he can "steer" any conversation towards cars, knows all the latest models, and has the best dad jokes!

Why did the dad become a movie buff?

Because he knows all the "blockbusters," can quote famous movie lines, and enjoys creating movie-themed jokes!

Why did the dad become a technology geek?

Because he's "wired" for humor, knows all the latest gadgets, and can "code" his way to laughter with tech jokes!

Why did the dad become a tech whiz?

Because he's always "wired" for humor, knows how to "debug" a funny situation, and can "program" laughter with his jokes!

Why did the dad become a foodie?

Because he savors the taste of a good joke, knows all the "spice" of humor, and can "dish" out laughter with every bite!

Why did the dad become a computer whiz?

Because he's the go-to person for tech support in the family, and he can "code" a hilarious punchline!

Why did the dad become a gardening expert?

Because he knows how to "dig" deep into gardening, nurture plants, and always finds a way to "grow" laughter!

Why did the dad become a BBQ master?

Because he's the "grill sergeant" of the backyard, knows how to "meat" expectations, and brings the flavor with dad jokes!

Why did the dad become a golf enthusiast?

Because he's always "teed up" for a good joke, knows how to "drive" home the punchline, and enjoys a round of laughter!

Why did the dad become a sports fanatic?

Because he knows how to "score" with his jokes, cheers for the winning team, and can "field" any humorous challenge!

Why did the dad become a fitness guru?

Because he knows how to "flex" his funny bone, has a "rep"-utation for humor, and can "workout" a good laugh!

Why did the dad become a musician?

Because he's got rhythm in his blood and can rock out on any instrument, especially the air guitar!

Why did the dad become a puzzle enthusiast?

Because he loves "piecing" things together, solving complex puzzles, and creating laughter with his wordplay!

Why did the dad become a puzzle solver?

Because he's a "mastermind" at solving puzzles, enjoys brain teasers, and always finds a way to "piece" together a joke!

Why did the dad become a travel enthusiast?

Because he's always "jet-set" for adventure, knows all the best travel tips, and can "map out" a path to laughter!

Why did the dad become a gardening pro?

Because he has a "green thumb" for comedy, knows how to "cultivate" laughter, and can "plant" jokes that bloom with humor!

Why did the dad become a pet lover?

Because he's always "paws-itively" funny, knows all the "tail"-telling jokes, and can "fetch" laughter with ease!

Why did the dad love to read mystery novels?

Because he's always been the detective of the family, solving problems and keeping everyone entertained!

Why did the dad become a foodie?

Because he knows the best restaurants in town, can grill up a mouthwatering feast, and always has a food pun!

Why did the dad become a music collector?

Because he loves "rocking" out to his favorite tunes, knows all the classic hits, and can "orchestrate" dad jokes!

Why did the dad become a fitness fanatic?

Because he knows how to "flex" his sense of humor, enjoys staying active, and can "work out" a good joke!

Why did the dad become a photography enthusiast?

Because he knows how to "capture" the perfect punchline, sees the world through a lens of humor, and can "develop" laughs!

Why did the dad become a music aficionado?

Because he knows how to "orchestrate" a great joke, has a "melody" of humor, and can "harmonize" laughter with style!

Why did the dad become a history buff?

Because he loves sharing fascinating historical facts and can make any history lesson fun and engaging!

Why did the dad become a travel enthusiast?

Because he loves exploring new destinations, making "dadventures," and discovering hidden jokes along the way!

Why did the dad become a pet lover?

Because he knows how to "paws" for a moment of laughter, enjoys funny pet anecdotes, and has a "tail-wagging" sense of humor!

Why did the dad become a puzzle master?

Because he loves to "piece" together a good joke, enjoys brain teasers, and can solve any puzzle with dad humor!

Why did the dad become a puzzle master?

Because he loves to "piece" together a good joke, enjoys brain teasers, and can solve any puzzle with dad humor!

Why did the dad become a fishing enthusiast?

Because he's "hooked" on jokes, knows all the "reel" punchlines, and can "catch" laughter like a pro angler!

Heartwarming Moments

Father's Day is a time to celebrate the love and appreciation we have for our dads. In this section, we take a break from the jokes and dive into heartwarming moments and memories. These moments will remind you of the kindness, wisdom, and unconditional love that fathers bring into our lives.

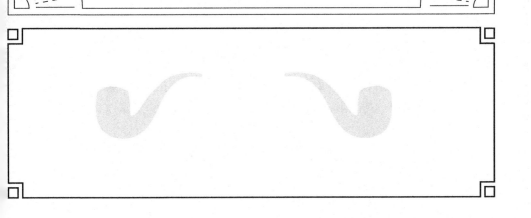

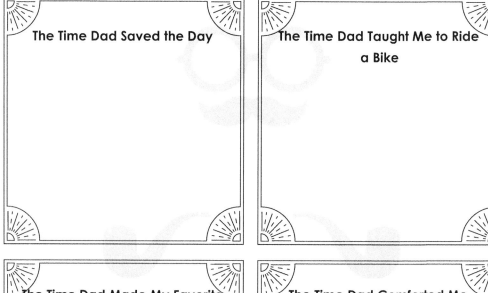

The Time Dad Saved the Day

The Time Dad Taught Me to Ride a Bike

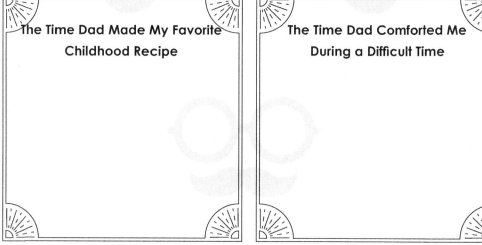

The Time Dad Made My Favorite Childhood Recipe

The Time Dad Comforted Me During a Difficult Time

The Time Dad Taught Me a Valuable Life Lesson

A Surprise Visit from Dad

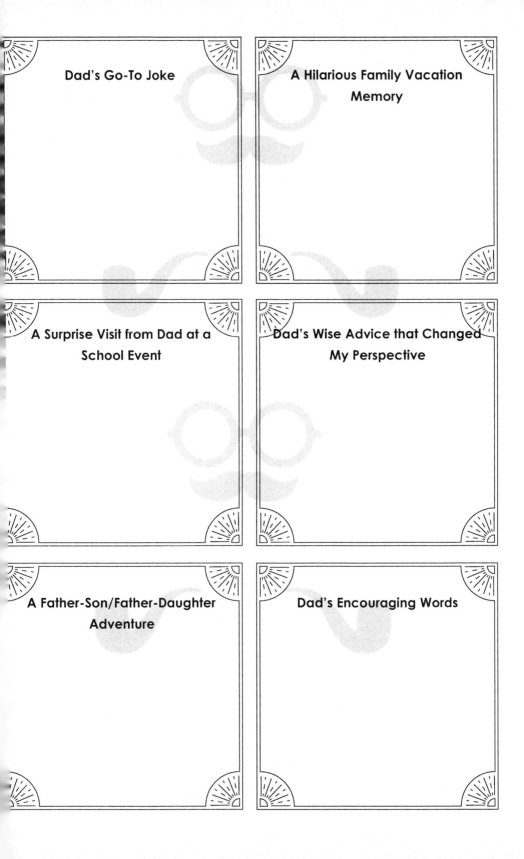

Dad's Go-To Joke

A Hilarious Family Vacation Memory

A Surprise Visit from Dad at a School Event

Dad's Wise Advice that Changed My Perspective

A Father-Son/Father-Daughter Adventure

Dad's Encouraging Words

Father-Daughter/Dad Moment

The Joy of Sharing a Favorite Hobby with Dad

A Silly Dance Party with Dad

A Special Father-Daughter/ Mother-Son Trip

Dad's Hilarious Dance Moves

A Family Tradition Passed Down from Dad

Dad's Hidden Talent

Dad's Support During a Difficult Time

Dad's Encouragement During a Sports Competition

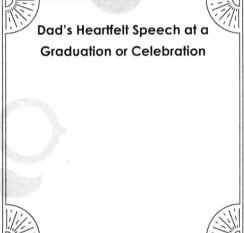

Dad's Heartfelt Speech at a Graduation or Celebration

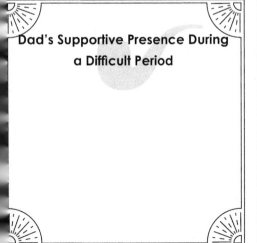

Dad's Supportive Presence During a Difficult Period

Dad's Wise and Funny Advice

Family Laughter

The Heartfelt Father-Daughter Dance

Building a Treehouse Together

A Surprise Gift or Gesture from Dad

The Joy of Making Dad Proud

Dad's Unconditional Love and Support

A Meaningful Gift from Dad

Creating Funny Traditions with Dad

A Memorable Road Trip with Dad

Dad's Proud Expression When I Achieved a Milestone

A Heartfelt Letter or Note from Dad

A Father-Daughter/Father-Son Bonding Experience

Dad's Comforting Presence in Times of Need

Celebrating Dad's Goofy Sense of Humor

The Joy of Watching Dad Play with Grandkids

The Joy of Sharing a Hobby or Interest with Dad

Dad's Silly Antics that Always Make Us Laugh

Dad's Heartfelt Speech or Toast

A Shared Hobby or Interest with Dad

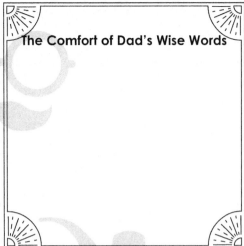

The Comfort of Dad's Wise Words

A Heartfelt Letter or Card from Dad

Dad's Unconditional Love and Support

Dad's Unwavering Belief in My Abilities

Dad's Thoughtful Gestures of Kindness

Dad's Support during Difficult Times

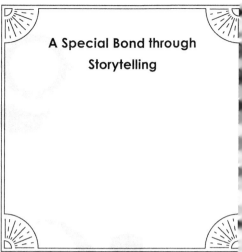

A Special Bond through Storytelling

Dad's Unwavering Support in Pursuing Dreams

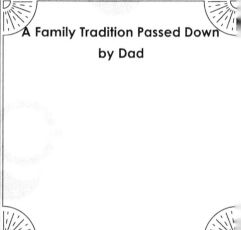

A Family Tradition Passed Down by Dad

The Comfort of Dad's Hugs

A Memorable Vacation with Dad

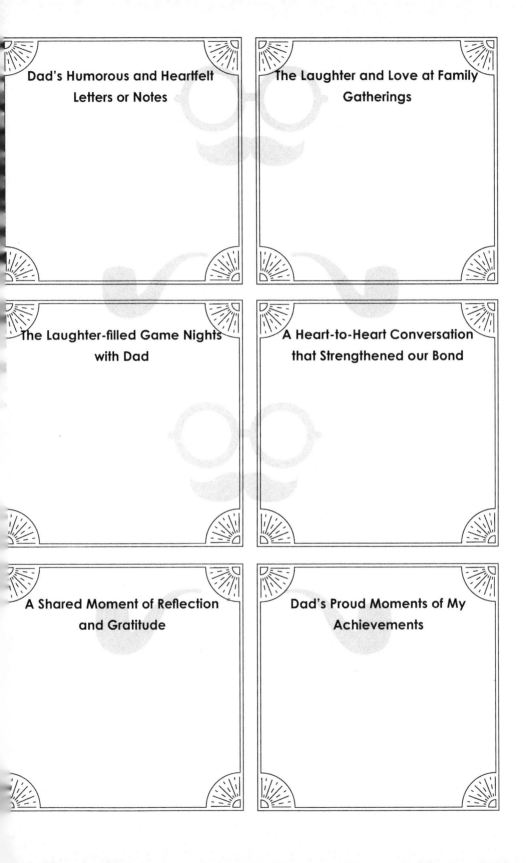

Dad's Humorous and Heartfelt Letters or Notes

The Laughter and Love at Family Gatherings

The Laughter-filled Game Nights with Dad

A Heart-to-Heart Conversation that Strengthened our Bond

A Shared Moment of Reflection and Gratitude

Dad's Proud Moments of My Achievements

A Special Father's Day Celebration

Dad's Unforgettable Parenting Lessons

A Surprise Family Reunion Arranged by Dad

Dad's Willingness to Listen and Understand

A Heart-to-Heart Conversation with Dad

Dad's Encouragement and Belief in Your Dreams

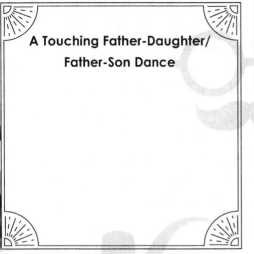

A Touching Father-Daughter/
Father-Son Dance

Dad's Sacrifices for Your Well-
being

A Surprise Visit or Gesture from
Dad

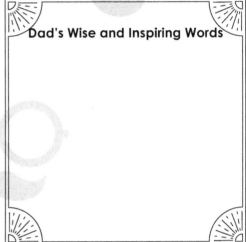

Dad's Wise and Inspiring Words

A Heartwarming Father-Child Trip
or Adventure

Dad's Unconditional Love and
Acceptance

Trivia Challenge

Test your knowledge and have some friendly competition with our Trivia Challenge section. Explore a wide range of interesting facts and questions that will keep you and your dad engaged and entertained. Get ready to showcase your trivia prowess and see who comes out on top!

Q1 : What is the official scientific term for "dad jokes"?

a) Paternal Paronomasia
b) Pater Puns
c) Dadplications
d) Father Funnies

Q2 : What do you call a group of dads competing in a barbecue contest?

a) The "Grilluminati"
b) The "Dad Squad"
c) The "Flame Fathers"
d) The "Sizzling Dads"

Q3 : What is a dad's favorite type of humor?

a) Puns
b) Slapstick
c) Sarcastic remarks
d) Dad jokes

Q4 : What do you call a dad's favorite reclining chair?

a) The "Dad Throne"
b) The "Lounger Deluxe"
c) The "Lazy Boy"
d) The "Relaxation Station"

Q 1:
What is the official scientific term for "dad jokes"?

a)
Paternal Paronomasia

Q 2:
What do you call a group of dads competing in a barbecue contest?

a)
The "Dad Squad"

Q 3:
What is a dad's favorite type of humor?

a)
Dad jokes

Q 4:
What do you call a dad's favorite reclining chair?

a)
The "Dad Throne"

Q1 : What is a group of dads called?

a) A "Gaggle"
b) A "Groan"
c) A "Quip-Quorum"
d) A "Pun-Demonium"

Q2 : How does a dad communicate with his kids on the internet?

a) He "Dadtexts"
b) He "Dadcodes"
c) He "Dadchats"
d) He "Dademojis"

Q3 : How does a dad make sure he never loses his keys?

a) He attaches them to a giant keychain
b) He memorizes the exact coordinates of their location
c) He hides a spare key under the doormat
d) He asks the kids to keep them safe

Q4 : How does a dad react when he hears a bad pun?

a) He laughs uncontrollably
b) He groans loudly
c) He rolls his eyes dramatically
d) He tells an even worse pun

Q 1:
What is a group of dads called?

a)
A "Groan"

Q 2:
How does a dad communicate with his kids on the internet?

a)
He "Dadtexts"

Q 3:
How does a dad make sure he never loses his keys?

a)
He attaches them to a giant keychain

Q 4:
How does a dad react when he hears a bad pun?

a)
He groans loudly

Q1 : How many "dad points" are earned when a dad successfully grills a perfect steak?

a) 100 dad points

b) 10,000 dad points

c) Dad points are incalculable...

d) Grilling a perfect steak is expected, no dad points awarded

---

Q2 : What is the official dad dance move at parties?

a) The "Dad Shuffle"

b) The "Dad Twist"

c) The "Dad Funk"

d) The "Dad Wiggle"

Q3 : What do you call a dad who takes his kids on adventurous outings?

a) The "AdventurDad"

b) The "Daring Daddy"

c) The "Exploration Extraordinaire"

d) The "Thrillseeking Father"

Q4 : What is a dad's preferred superpower?

a) The ability to grill the perfect burger

b) The power to fix anything with duct tape

c) The skill to embarrass their children in public

d) The talent to fall asleep anywhere

Q 1:
How many "dad points" are earned when a dad successfully grills a perfect steak?

a)
Dad points are incalculable, they transcend mathematics

Q 2:
What is the official dad dance move at parties?

a)
The "Dad Shuffle"

Q 3:
What do you call a dad who takes his kids on adventurous outings?

a)
The "AdventurDad"

Q 4:
What is a dad's preferred superpower?

a)
The power to fix anything with duct tape

Q1 : What is the favorite dance move of dads at weddings?

a) The Dad Slide
b) The Dad Shuffle
c) The Dad Dab
d) The Dad Wave

Q2 : How does a dad keep his cool during stressful situations?

a) He uses his "Dad Reflexes"
b) He takes deep breaths and counts to 10
c) He imagines himself on a tropical island
d) He makes terrible dad jokes

Q3 : How does a dad stay in shape?

a) He mows the lawn using only a manual push mower
b) He runs after his kids in the park
c) He participates in the annual "Dad Olympics"
d) He attends "Dad Bootcamp" classes

Q4 : What do you call a dad's favorite tool for fixing things around the house?

a) The "Fix-It Wand"
b) The "Magic Screwdriver"
c) The "Handy Hammer"
d) The "Dad Toolbelt"

Q 1:
What is the favorite dance move of dads at weddings?

a)
The Dad Slide

Q 2:
How does a dad keep his cool during stressful situations?

a)
He uses his "Dad Reflexes"

Q 3:
How does a dad stay in shape?

a)
He runs after his kids in the park

Q 4:
What do you call a dad's favorite tool for fixing things around the house?

a)
The "Magic Screwdriver"

Q1 : According to the "Dad Code," what is the appropriate response when someone asks, "Are we there yet?"

a) We'll get there when we get there!

b) Only ten more minutes!

c) No, we're actually going the long way around.

d) We've been there all along, it's the journey that matters.

Q2 : What is a dad's favorite tool for grilling?

a) The "Flippin' Fantastic"

b) The "Meat Master 3000"

c) The "Grillinator"

d) The "BBQ Wizard"

Q3 : What is a dad's favorite movie genre?

a) Action-comedies

b) Westerns

c) Romantic comedies

d) Superhero movies

Q4 : How does a dad handle technology issues?

a) He presses random buttons until something works

b) He asks his kids for help

c) He resorts to using outdated devices

d) He blames the technology for not understanding him

Q 1:
According to the "Dad Code," what is the appropriate response when someone asks, "Are we there

a)
We've been there all along, it's the journey that matters.

Q 2:
What is a dad's favorite tool for grilling?

a)
The "Grillinator"

Q 3:
What is a dad's favorite movie genre?

a)
Action-comedies

Q 4:
How does a dad handle technology issues?

a)
He presses random buttons until something works

Q1 : What is the primary ingredient in a dad's secret recipe sauce?

a) Ketchup

b) Mustard

c) Worcestershire sauce

d) Love and bad puns

Q2 : How does a dad wake up in the morning?

a) With a "Dad-alarm"

b) With a "Dad Roar"

c) With a "Dad Joke"

d) With a "Dad Dance"

Q3 : How does a dad handle a spider in the house?

a) He calls for backup from the family cat

b) He attempts to negotiate a peaceful relocation

c) He uses a glass and a piece of paper to catch and release it

d) He screams for help and runs away

Q4 : What is a dad's favorite TV show genre?

a) Crime dramas

b) Home improvement shows

c) Sports broadcasts

d) Sitcoms

Q 1:
What is the primary ingredient in a dad's secret recipe sauce?

a)
Love and bad puns

Q 2:
How does a dad wake up in the morning?

a)
With a "Dad Joke"

Q 3:
How does a dad handle a spider in the house?

a)
He attempts to negotiate a peaceful relocation

Q 4:
What is a dad's favorite TV show genre?

a)
Home improvement shows

Q1 : What is the dad superpower that allows them to locate lost items?

a) X-ray vision

b) Telepathy

c) The ability to summon the item with a loud shout

d) The "dad sense" that comes from years of experience

Q2 : What is a dad's go-to karaoke song?

a) Sweet Home Alabama

b) Bohemian Rhapsody

c) I Will Survive

d) Dancing Queen

Q3 : What is a dad's signature dish in the kitchen?

a) Dad's Famous Chili

b) Grilled Cheese Delight

c) Spaghetti Surprise

d) Microwave Masterpiece

Q4 : How does a dad react when his favorite sports team loses?

a) He pretends it doesn't bother him, but secretly sulks for days

b) He throws a mini tantrum and yells at the TV

c) He analyzes the game and criticizes the referee's decisions

d) He blames the loss on superstitions or bad luck

Q 1: What is the dad superpower that allows them to locate lost items?	Q 2: What is a dad's go-to karaoke song?	Q 3: What is a dad's signature dish in the kitchen?	Q 4: How does a dad react when his favorite sports team loses?
a) The ability to summon the item with a loud shout	a) Sweet Home Alabama	a) Dad's Famous Chili	a) He pretends it doesn't bother him, but secretly sulks for

Q1 : What is the dad-approved solution for any household problem?

a) Duct tape

b) WD-40

c) A combination of both

d) Calling a professional

Q2 : How does a dad ensure he never runs out of dad jokes?

a) He keeps a "Dad Joke Jar"

b) He subscribes to a "Joke-a-Day" service

c) He has a "Dad Joke Rolodex"

d) He's a member of the "International Dad Joke Society"

Q3 : What is a dad's favorite mode of transportation?

a) The minivan

b) The classic station wagon

c) The trusty bicycle

d) The motorized lawnmower

Q4 : What is a dad's preferred mode of transportation when he's in a hurry?

a) The dad jog

b) The speed walk

c) The power walk

d) The dad sprint

Q 1: What is the dad-approved solution for any household problem? **a)** **Duct tape**	Q 2: How does a dad ensure he never runs out of dad jokes? **a)** **He subscribes to a "Joke-a-Day" service**	Q 3: What is a dad's favorite mode of transportation? **a)** **The minivan**	Q 4: What is a dad's preferred mode of transportation when he's in a hurry? **a)** **The dad jog**

DIY Project

Unleash your creativity and embark on a DIY adventure with your dad in our DIY Project section. Discover fun and exciting projects that you can work on together, creating lasting memories and unique handmade items that celebrate your father-child bond.

DIY Project:

Customized Wooden Phone Stand

Materials needed:

Wooden board or plank (approximately 8x4 inches)
Saw or miter saw
Sandpaper (medium and fine grit)
Wood stain or paint (optional)
Paintbrush or sponge
Ruler or measuring tape
Pencil
Wood glue or strong adhesive
Clamps (optional)
Clear varnish or sealant (optional)
Felt pads (optional)

Start by selecting a wooden board or plank that is suitable for the phone stand. You can choose a hardwood like oak or walnut for durability, or use a softer wood like pine for a more rustic look.

Measure and mark the dimensions for the phone stand on the wooden board. A common size is approximately 8 inches in length and 4 inches in width. Adjust the measurements to fit your father's preferences.

Use a saw or miter saw to carefully cut along the marked lines to create the base and back of the phone stand. Take your time and ensure the cuts are straight and even.

Once the pieces are cut, use sandpaper with medium grit to smooth any rough edges or surfaces. Then, switch to a fine grit sandpaper to further refine the wood's finish.

If desired, apply wood stain or paint to the wooden pieces. Follow the instructions on the stain or paint container and allow it to dry completely.

Apply a thin layer of wood glue or strong adhesive to one edge of the base piece. Position the back piece perpendicular to the base and press them firmly together. Use clamps if necessary to hold the pieces in place while the adhesive dries.

Allow the adhesive to dry completely according to the instructions provided by the glue manufacturer.

Optional: Apply a clear varnish or sealant to protect the wood and enhance its appearance. This step will give the phone stand a polished and professional look.

Once the varnish or sealant is dry, your customized wooden phone stand is ready to use.

Optional: Attach small felt pads to the bottom corners of the phone stand to prevent it from scratching surfaces or sliding.

Present the DIY phone stand to your father as a thoughtful and functional gift. He can use it to hold his phone while charging, watching videos, or following recipes in the kitchen.

Note: This project can be adapted to other interests or hobbies by adding personalized touches. For example, if your father is a sports fan, you could incorporate his favorite team's logo or colors into the design using paint, decals, or woodburning techniques.

DIY Project:

Personalized Father's Day Photo Album

Materials needed:

Photo album or scrapbook
Decorative papers or cardstock
Scissors
Glue or adhesive
Photos of special moments with your father
Markers or pens
Stickers or embellishments (optional)

.Select a photo album or scrapbook that suits your father's style or preferences
.Gather photos of special moments with your father, such as family vacations, birthdays, or holidays
.Cut decorative papers or cardstock into various shapes and sizes to create unique backgrounds for your photos
.Arrange the photos on each page, leaving space for written captions or notes
.Use glue or adhesive to secure the photos and decorative papers onto the pages
.Write heartfelt messages, captions, or memories beside each photo using markers or pens
.Get creative with additional embellishments such as stickers, ribbons, or themed decorations to enhance the pages
.Personalize the cover of the photo album with your father's name, a special title, or a meaningful quote
.Allow the glue to dry completely before handling or presenting the DIY photo album to your father
Present the completed photo album to your father on Father's Day, and enjoy reminiscing together about the cherished
.moments captured in the album

Note: Feel free to adapt this DIY project based on your father's interests or hobbies. For example, if he enjoys gardening, you could create a personalized gardening journal or design custom plant markers instead of a photo album.

Father-Child Bonding Activities

Strengthen the bond with your dad through a series of interactive and engaging activities designed to bring you closer together. From outdoor adventures to shared hobbies, these activities will create meaningful connections and provide opportunities for quality time and laughter.

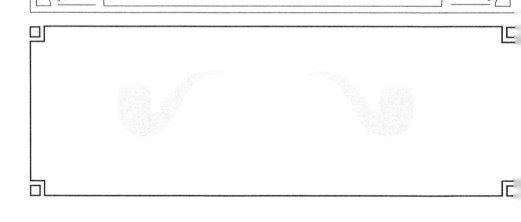

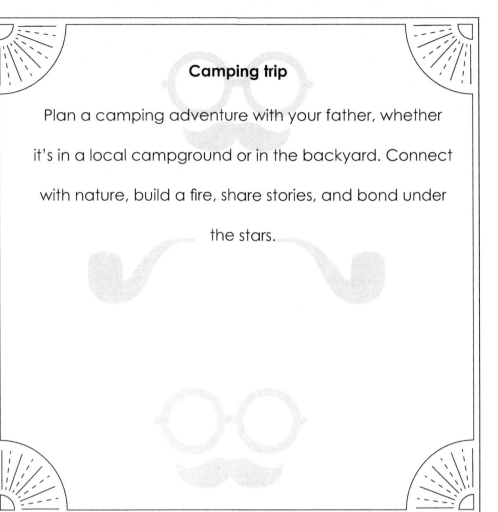

Camping trip

Plan a camping adventure with your father, whether it's in a local campground or in the backyard. Connect with nature, build a fire, share stories, and bond under the stars.

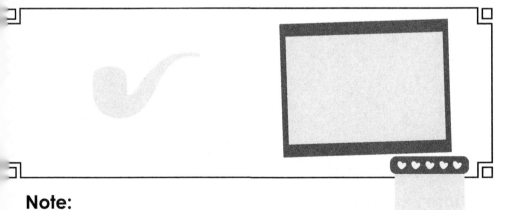

Note:

Art project

Engage in a creative art project together, such as painting, sculpting, or crafting. Explore your artistic sides, encourage each other's creativity, and create unique pieces of art while enjoying quality time.

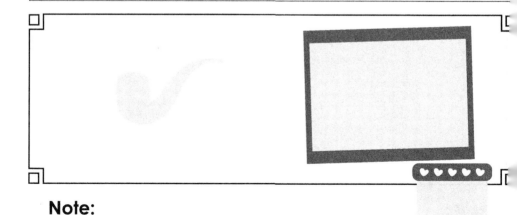

Note:

Sports day

Organize a sports day where you and your father can play your favorite sports or try out new ones. It can be anything from basketball, soccer, or even a game of catch in the backyard. Strengthen your bond through friendly competition and shared passion for sports.

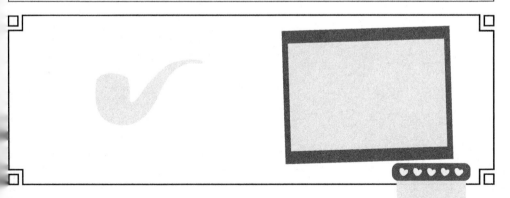

Note:

Book club

Start a father-child book club where you both read the same book and discuss it together. Choose books that interest both of you, and exchange thoughts, insights, and recommendations. This activity promotes literacy, critical thinking, and shared intellectual growth.

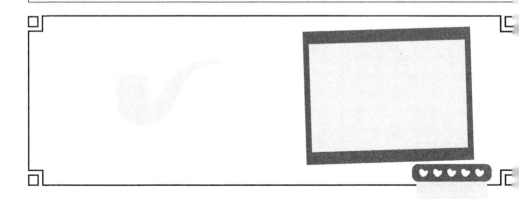

Note:

DIY science experiments

Conduct hands-on science experiments at home,

exploring topics like physics, chemistry, or biology.

Learn together, marvel at scientific phenomena,

and ignite curiosity through fun and educational

experiments.

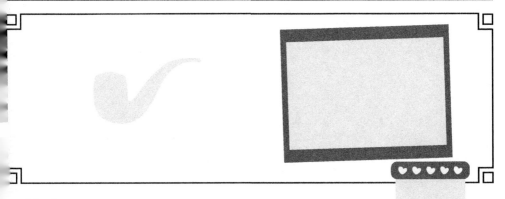

Note:

Music jam session

If you and your father enjoy music, have a jam session

together. Play your instruments, sing songs, and share

your favorite tunes. It's a fantastic way to express

yourselves, collaborate, and enjoy the power of music.

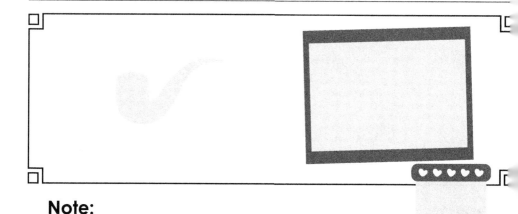

Note:

Photography excursion

Go on a photography excursion with your father,

exploring your surroundings and capturing moments

through the lens. Share your perspectives, learn about

composition and lighting, and create a visual diary of

your adventures.

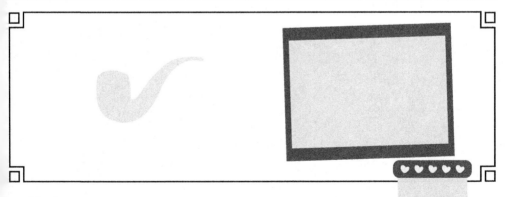

Note:

Gardening

Start a garden together, whether it's a small herb garden or a backyard vegetable patch. Nurture plants, learn about nature, and witness the fruits of your labor as you cultivate a shared space of beauty and growth.

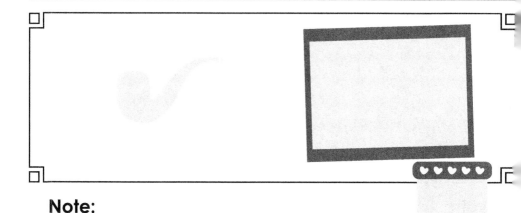

Note:

Puzzle-solving challenge

Choose a challenging puzzle, such as a jigsaw puzzle

or a brain-teasing riddle. Work together to solve it,

exercising your problem-solving skills, teamwork, and

patience. Enjoy the satisfaction of cracking the puzzle

as a team.

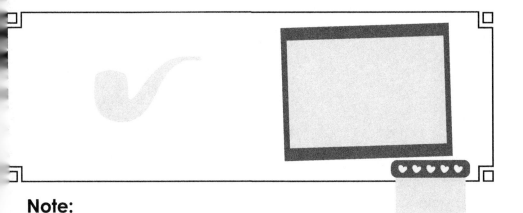

Note:

Road trip adventure

Plan a road trip with your father to explore new places, visit landmarks, or embark on a spontaneous adventure. Bond during the journey, share stories, and create unforgettable memories while discovering new destinations.

Note:

Outdoor Adventure Day

Spend a day together in nature by going on a hike,

exploring a local park, or having a picnic in a scenic

spot. Engaging in outdoor activities allows you to

connect with each other while enjoying the beauty

of the natural world. It provides an opportunity for

meaningful conversations, shared experiences, and

creating lasting memories.

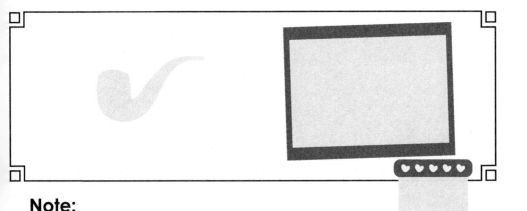

Note:

Movie Marathon

Plan a movie marathon featuring your father's favorite films or a series that both of you enjoy. Snuggle up on the couch with some popcorn and snacks, and immerse yourselves in a cinematic journey together. This activity not only offers entertainment but also opens the door for discussions about the movies, sharing your thoughts and emotions, and discovering new aspects of each other's tastes.

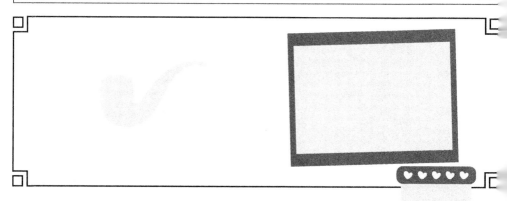

Note:

Cooking Adventure

Set aside a day to cook a meal together from scratch.

Choose a recipe that both you and your father are

interested in trying. Collaborating in the kitchen allows

you to bond while learning valuable cooking skills and

exploring new flavors. From chopping vegetables

to stirring the pots, the shared effort in preparing a

delicious meal can foster teamwork and create a

sense of accomplishment.

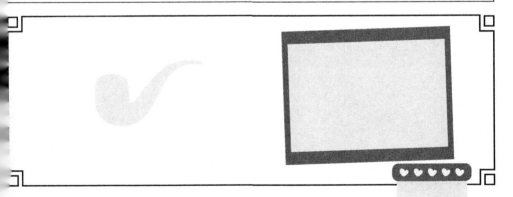

Note:

Sports or Game Day

Engage in a friendly sports match or play board games or video games together. Whether it's shooting hoops in the backyard, playing a round of chess, or competing in a video game tournament, these activities promote healthy competition, communication, and laughter. They provide an opportunity for bonding through shared interests and the joy of friendly rivalry.

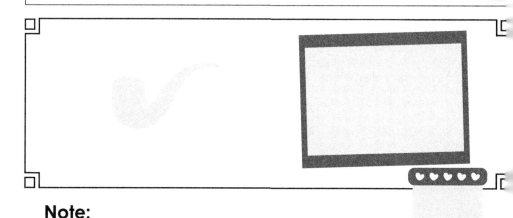

Note:

Volunteer or Community Service

Engage in a volunteer or community service activity together. Find a local organization or cause that aligns with both your interests, such as a food bank, animal shelter, or environmental cleanup. Participating in acts of service as a team teaches the value of giving back, cultivates empathy, and strengthens your bond by working towards a common goal for the betterment of your community.

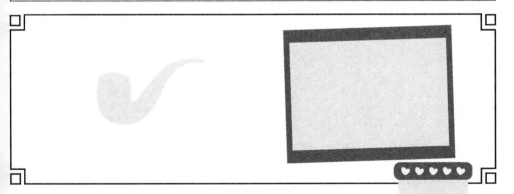

Note:

Riddle Challenge

Get your thinking caps on for our Riddle Challenge section. Put your problem-solving skills to the test with a collection of mind-boggling riddles that will challenge you and your dad. From logical puzzles to brain teasers, this section guarantees a lot of fun and mental stimulation.

I have keys but no locks. I have space but no room. You can enter, but you can't go outside. What am I?

**Answer:
A keyboard**

I speak without a mouth and hear without ears. I have no body, but I come alive with wind. What am I?

**Answer:
An echo**

I have keys but can't open any doors. I have space but no physical form. People come to me seeking answers. What am I?

**Answer:
A computer**

I have keys but can't open locks. I have space but no room. You can enter, but you can't go outside. What am I?

**Answer:
A piano**

I am taken from a mine and shut in a wooden case. From far away, I am sought after. What am I?

**Answer:
Pencil lead**

I can be cracked, made, told, and played. I can bring laughter or tears. What am I?

**Answer:
A joke**

I can fly without wings. I can cry without eyes. Wherever I go, darkness follows me. What am I?

Answer:
A cloud

What has keys but can't open locks?

Answer:
A piano

I have a face that doesn't frown, hands that don't wave, and yet I tell a story. What am I?

Answer:
A clock

I have a heart that doesn't beat. I have a home but I never sleep. I can take a man's house and build another's. And I love to play games with my many brothers. What am I?

Answer:
The ocean

I am full of holes, yet I can hold water. What am I?

Answer:
A sponge

I am full of holes, but I can still hold water. What am I?

Answer:
A sponge

I speak without a mouth and hear without ears. I have a body, but I'm invisible. What am I?

**Answer:
A thought**

The more you take, the more you leave behind. What am I?

**Answer:
Footsteps**

I have a neck but no head. I have a body but no arms or legs. I can be easily tied yet cannot be untied. What am I?

**Answer:
A shirt**

I have cities but no buildings, forests but no trees, and rivers but no water. What am I?

**Answer:
A book**

The more you have of me, the less you see. What am I?

**Answer:
Darkness**

I have cities but no people, forests but no trees, and rivers but no water. What am I?

**Answer:
A globe**

The more you take, the more you leave behind. What am I?

Answer:
Footsteps

I have cities but no houses, forests but no trees, and rivers but no water. What am I?

Answer:
A map

I have branches, but no leaves. I hold water, but I'm not a cup. What am I?

Answer:
A river

I can be cracked, made, told, and played. What am I?

Answer:
A joke

I can fly without wings, cry without eyes, and run without legs. What am I?

Answer:
Clouds

I have a head and a tail, but no body. I can be found in the sky or on your dining table. What am I?

Answer:
A coin

I have cities but no houses, forests but no trees, and rivers but no water. What am I?

**Answer:
A map**

What has a heart that doesn't beat?

**Answer:
A deck of cards**

I have keys but can't open any locks. I have space but no rooms. Every day, you enter me, yet you never leave. What am I?

**Answer:
A calendar**

I am taken from a mine and shut in a wooden case from which I'm never released. Yet, I am used by almost every person. What am I?

**Answer:
Pencil lead/graphite**

I have keys but no locks. I have space but no room. You can enter but can't go outside. What am I?

**Answer:
A keyboard**

I am taken from a mine and shut in a wooden case. When released, I can shine with brilliance. What am I?

**Answer:
A diamond**

Fun Facts

Dive into a world of fascinating and entertaining facts in our Fun Facts section. Explore a wide range of topics and discover intriguing information that will leave you and your dad amazed and entertained. From little-known trivia to surprising insights, you're in for a treat!

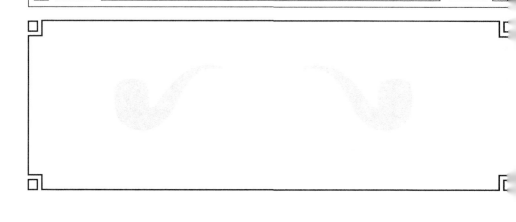

Fun Fact 1 :

According to a study by the University of Oxford, children tend to inherit their intelligence from their mothers. However, the study also emphasized that fathers play a crucial role in shaping a child's educational attainment and career choices.

Fun Fact 2 :

The world's oldest known musical instrument is a flute made from a vulture's wing bone, dating back over 40,000 years.

Fun Fact 3 :

The universe is so vast that there are more stars in the universe than grains of sand on all the beaches on Earth combined.

Fun Fact 4 :

The world's oldest father is believed to be Ramjit Raghav from India, who fathered his first child at the age of 94.

Fun Fact 5 :

The word "dad" is often one of the first words a baby learns to say. It is considered one of the easiest sounds for babies to pronounce.

Fun Fact 6 :

Father's Day is celebrated on different dates worldwide. While it is widely celebrated on the third Sunday in June, some countries, such as Australia and New Zealand, celebrate it in September.

Fun Fact 1 :

In a survey conducted by Netflix, 75% of dads admitted to having pretended to understand a TV show or movie their child was talking about, even though they had no idea what it was.

Fun Fact 2 :

The Sahara Desert, the largest hot desert in the world, is expanding and has grown by around 10% in the past century.

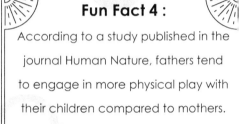

Fun Fact 3 :

Honey never spoils. Archaeologists have discovered pots of honey in ancient Egyptian tombs that are over 3,000 years old and still perfectly edible.

Fun Fact 4 :

According to a study published in the journal Human Nature, fathers tend to engage in more physical play with their children compared to mothers.

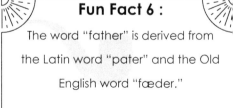

Fun Fact 5 :

The world's tallest father is Sultan Kösen from Turkey, who stands at a height of 8 feet 2.8 inches (251 cm).

Fun Fact 6 :

The word "father" is derived from the Latin word "pater" and the Old English word "fæder."

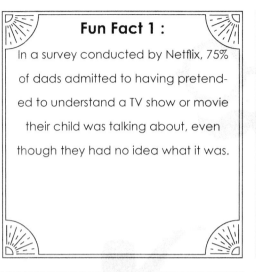

Fun Fact 1 :

The average age of fathers in the United States has been steadily increasing over the years. In 1972, the average age of a new father was 27.4 years old. By 2015, it had risen to 30.9 years old.

Fun Fact 2 :

The deepest part of the ocean, the Mariana Trench, is deeper than Mount Everest is tall. It reaches a depth of about 36,070 feet (10,994 meters).

Fun Fact 3 :

The Great Wall of China, often re-garded as one of the Seven Wonders of the World, is visible from space, but only under certain weather condi-tions.

Fun Fact 4 :

The fictional character James Bond, known for his suave personality and action-packed adventures, became a father in the 2006 film "Casino Royale" when it was revealed that he had a daughter.

Fun Fact 5 :

A study published in the journal Pediatrics found that children who have involved fathers are less likely to engage in risky behaviors.

Fun Fact 6 :

The world's oldest known father was a man named Les Colley from Australia, who fathered a child at the age of 92 in 1998.

Fun Fact 1 :

Studies have shown that fathers who actively participate in childcare and household tasks have children who perform better academically and have higher levels of emotional well-being.

Fun Fact 2 :

There is a species of jellyfish, known as Turritopsis dohrnii, that is biologically immortal and can revert its cells back to their earliest form.

Fun Fact 3 :

Octopuses have the ability to change both the color and texture of their skin, allowing them to blend seamlessly with their surroundings.

Fun Fact 4 :

Father's Day is celebrated on different dates around the world. In Germany, it is celebrated on Ascension Day, while in Australia, it is observed on the first Sunday in September.

Fun Fact 5 :

The concept of a "father-daughter dance" at weddings dates back to ancient Roman times when fathers would dance with their daughters to symbolize the transfer of responsibility from father to husband.

Fun Fact 6 :

A study conducted by the National Institutes of Health found that children who have involved fathers are more likely to have better physical and mental health outcomes.

Fun Fact 1 :

In a survey conducted by Parents Magazine, 71% of fathers admitted to singing lullabies to their children. Many fathers find it a soothing and bonding experience, despite their singing skills!

Fun Fact 2 :

The average person walks the equivalent of three times around the world in their lifetime.

Fun Fact 3 :

The human brain is capable of generating more electrical impulses in a single day than all the telephones in the world combined.

Fun Fact 4 :

The famous physicist Albert Einstein became a father twice, having two sons named Hans and Eduard. Despite his groundbreaking scientific achievements, Einstein expressed that being a father brought him the greatest joy.

Fun Fact 5 :

The famous painter Pablo Picasso was a father to four children, each of whom inspired and influenced his artwork in different ways.

Fun Fact 6 :

The role of fathers in parenting has evolved over time. In recent decades, there has been a shift towards more active and engaged fatherhood, with dads taking on more caregiving responsibilities.

Fun Fact 1 :

The longest recorded human pregnancy was 375 days (approximately 12.5 months). While this is an exceptional case, the average length of pregnancy is around 280 days (or 40 weeks).

Fun Fact 2 :

The world's largest cave, Son Doong Cave in Vietnam, is so big that it has its own river, jungle, and cloud formations inside.

Fun Fact 3 :

Mount Everest, the highest peak on Earth, continues to grow by about a quarter of an inch every year due to tectonic plate movements.

Fun Fact 4 :

A study published in the journal Pediatrics found that children who have positive and involved relationships with their fathers are less likely to experience depression and anxiety later in life.

Fun Fact 5 :

Research has shown that fathers who engage in rough-and-tumble play with their children contribute to their emotional and social development.

Fun Fact 6 :

Did you know that the longest recorded distance for a paper airplane flight is 226 feet and 10 inches? You and your father can have fun making and testing different paper airplane designs.

Fun Fact 1 :

Did you know that the term "dad joke" has become a popular phrase? Dad jokes are known for their cheesy and often pun-filled humor that elicit groans and eye-rolls from their children. Embrace the dad joke culture!

Fun Fact 2 :

The human eye can distinguish approximately 10 million different colors.

Fun Fact 3 :

The world's oldest known living organism is a grove of aspen trees in Utah, USA, named Pando. It is estimated to be over 80,000 years old.

Fun Fact 4 :

The famous inventor Thomas Edison, known for his numerous patents and contributions to modern technology, was a father to six children. His youngest son, Theodore, went on to become a successful inventor and businessman as well.

Fun Fact 5 :

The world's largest gathering of fathers is known as the "World's Greatest Dad's Day." It takes place annually in Washington, D.C., and brings together thousands of fathers and their families for a day of celebration and activities.

Fun Fact 6 :

The famous physicist Albert Einstein became a father twice in his lifetime. He had a daughter named Lieserl and two sons named Hans and Eduard.

Fun Fact 1 :

Fathers play an essential role in language development. Research has found that the more fathers engage in playful and interactive conversations with their infants, the more their children's language skills develop.

Fun Fact 2 :

The hummingbird is the only bird that can fly backward and hover in mid-air.

Fun Fact 3 :

There are more possible iterations of a game of chess than there are atoms in the known universe.

Fun Fact 4 :

Father's Day is celebrated in over 80 countries worldwide, although the dates may vary. It is a day dedicated to honoring and appreciating fathers and father figures for their love, guidance, and support.

Fun Fact 5 :

The average number of children per father varies across countries. In Nigeria, for example, the average number is 7.09 children per father, while in Japan, it is 1.42 children per father.

Fun Fact 6 :

Father's Day is not only celebrated for biological fathers but also for father figures such as stepfathers, adoptive fathers, and grandfathers. It is a day to honor all those who play a significant role in a child's life.

Fun Fact 1 :

The concept of Father's Day dates back to 1909 when Sonora Smart Dodd, inspired by Mother's Day, advocated for a day to honor fathers. The first official Father's Day was celebrated on June 19, 1910, in Spokane, Washington.

Fun Fact 2 :

The Amazon Rainforest produces more than 20% of the world's oxygen and is often referred to as the "lungs of the Earth."

Fun Fact 3 :

The world's largest living structure is the Great Barrier Reef, stretching over 2,300 kilometers (1,400 miles) along the coast of Australia.

Fun Fact 4 :

According to the Guinness World Records, the largest gathering of fathers and their children took place in 2019 in the Philippines, with over 50,000 participants. The event aimed to promote the importance of fatherhood and strengthen family bonds.

Fun Fact 5 :

The role of fathers in childbirth has evolved over time. Today, many fathers actively participate in the delivery room, providing support and encouragement to their partners during the birthing process.

Fun Fact 6 :

The relationship between a father and child can have a significant impact on a child's self-esteem and social development. Positive father-child relationships have been linked to higher levels of confidence and better relationships with others.

Fun Fact 1 :

Did you know that actor and former California governor Arnold Schwarzenegger holds the record for the highest salary earned for a single film? He received a staggering $29.25 million for his role in the 1994 film "True Lies."

Fun Fact 2 :

The Earth's core is hotter than the surface of the Sun, reaching temperatures of up to 9,932 degrees Fahrenheit (5,500 degrees Celsius).

Fun Fact 3 :

Your nose can remember over 50,000 different scents, making it one of the most powerful and sensitive organs in the human body.

Fun Fact 4 :

In many cultures, fathers play a significant role in passing down traditions, values, and skills to their children. This includes teaching them important life lessons, imparting knowledge, and providing guidance as they navigate through various stages of life.

Fun Fact 5 :

In some cultures, fathers have special traditions or rituals associated with childbirth and child-rearing. For example, in Japan, there is a tradition called "Shichigosan" where fathers take their children to a shrine at the ages of three, five, and seven to pray for their well-being and growth.

Fun Fact 6 :

Did you know that the famous poet Robert Frost was a father to six children? His experiences as a father often influenced his poetry, which explored themes of family and nature.

Reflective Questions

Take a moment of introspection and deep conversation with our Reflective Questions section. Explore meaningful topics, share your thoughts, and engage in heartfelt discussions that will strengthen your bond and help you gain a deeper understanding of each other.

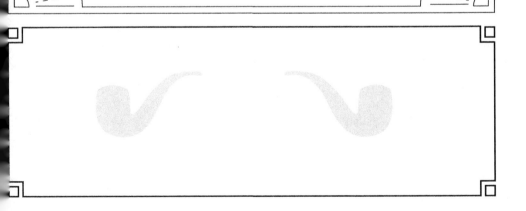

Reflective Question 1 :

What has been the most rewarding

part of being a father?

Additional Information 1 :

Reflect on specific moments, ex-

periences, or milestones that have

brought you immense joy, pride, or a

sense of fulfillment as a father.

Reflective Question 2 :

What is the most important lesson you

want to teach your children?

Additional Information 1 :

Reflect on the values, skills, or life

lessons that you consider essential

to pass on to your children, and why

you believe they are important for

their growth and development.

Reflective Question 3 :

How do you foster a sense of belong-

ing and inclusion within your family?

Additional Information 1 :

Explore the ways in which you create

an environment where every family

member feels valued, heard, and

accepted.

Reflective Question 1 :

In what ways has fatherhood

changed you?

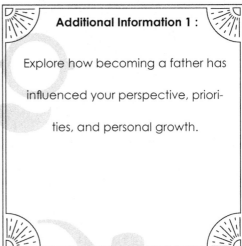

Additional Information 1 :

Explore how becoming a father has

influenced your perspective, priori-

ties, and personal growth.

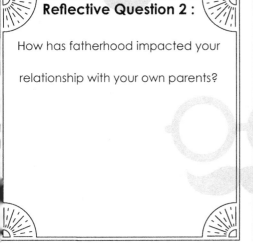

Reflective Question 2 :

How has fatherhood impacted your

relationship with your own parents?

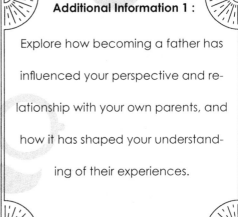

Additional Information 1 :

Explore how becoming a father has

influenced your perspective and re-

lationship with your own parents, and

how it has shaped your understand-

ing of their experiences.

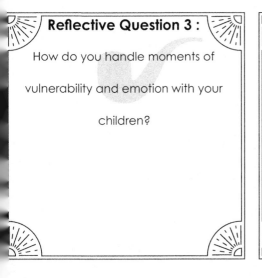

Reflective Question 3 :

How do you handle moments of

vulnerability and emotion with your

children?

Additional Information 1 :

Reflect on how you navigate conver-

sations about emotions and create

a safe space for your children to

express themselves openly.

Reflective Question 1 :

What lessons have you learned from

your own father that you've applied

in your own parenting?

Additional Information 1 :

Reflect on the values, teachings, or

parenting approaches that you have

inherited from your own father and

how they have shaped your journey

as a dad.

Reflective Question 2 :

What role does communication play

in your relationship with your chil-

dren?

Additional Information 1 :

Consider the importance of open

and effective communication in

building a strong connection with

your children, and how you actively

foster a communicative environment.

Reflective Question 3 :

How do you encourage and support

your children's unique talents and

interests?

Additional Information 1 :

Consider how you identify and

nurture your children's individual

strengths and passions, and the ways

in which you provide opportunities for

them to develop and explore their

interests.

Reflective Question 1 :

What challenges have you faced as a father, and how have you overcome them?

Additional Information 1 :

Share your experiences and reflect on the obstacles you have encountered along the way, as well as the strategies or support systems that helped you overcome them.

Reflective Question 2 :

What strategies do you use to handle moments of stress or frustration as a father?

Additional Information 1 :

Reflect on the coping mechanisms, self-care practices, or strategies you employ to manage stress or frustration and maintain a positive mindset as a father.

Reflective Question 3 :

What role does humor play in your relationship with your children?

Additional Information 1 :

Reflect on the importance of laughter and humor in building connections, diffusing tension, and creating joyful memories with your children.

Reflective Question 1 :

How do you balance being a father with your other roles and responsibilities?

Additional Information 1 :

Consider the various roles and responsibilities you have in life and reflect on how you strive to find a balance between being a father and fulfilling other obligations.

Reflective Question 2 :

How do you encourage independence and growth in your children while still providing guidance and support?

Additional Information 1 :

Explore the balance between giving your children space to develop their independence and providing them with the necessary guidance and support as they navigate life's challenges.

Reflective Question 3 :

How do you teach your children the value of empathy and compassion towards others?

Additional Information 1 :

Explore the ways in which you instill empathy and compassion in your children, such as through modeling, teaching by example, and encouraging acts of kindness and understanding.

Reflective Question 1 :

What do you hope your children will remember most about their childhood and your role as their father?

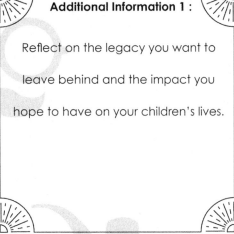

Additional Information 1 :

Reflect on the legacy you want to leave behind and the impact you hope to have on your children's lives.

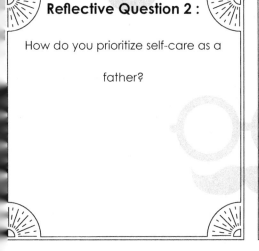

Reflective Question 2 :

How do you prioritize self-care as a father?

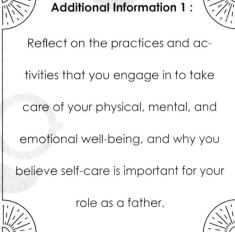

Additional Information 1 :

Reflect on the practices and activities that you engage in to take care of your physical, mental, and emotional well-being, and why you believe self-care is important for your role as a father.

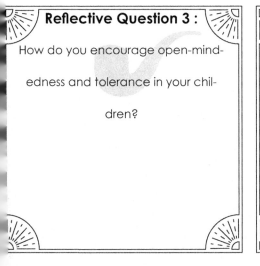

Reflective Question 3 :

How do you encourage open-mindedness and tolerance in your children?

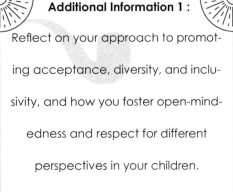

Additional Information 1 :

Reflect on your approach to promoting acceptance, diversity, and inclusivity, and how you foster open-mindedness and respect for different perspectives in your children.

Reflective Question 1 :

How have you grown as a parent since the birth of your first child?

Additional Information 1 :

Reflect on the changes you have witnessed in your parenting style, knowledge, and confidence as you gained experience over time.

Reflective Question 2 :

How do you handle conflicts or disagreements with your children in a constructive and respectful manner?

Additional Information 1 :

Consider your approach to resolving conflicts or disagreements with your children, emphasizing the importance of active listening, empathy, and finding common ground.

Reflective Question 3 :

How do you navigate and teach your children about the importance of boundaries and personal space?

Additional Information 1 :

Consider how you guide your children in understanding and respecting personal boundaries, both for themselves and others, to foster healthy relationships and self-awareness.

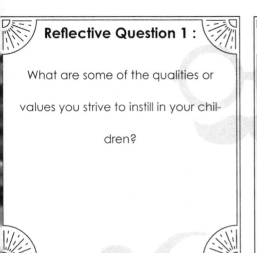

Reflective Question 1 :

What are some of the qualities or values you strive to instill in your children?

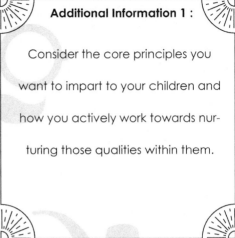

Additional Information 1 :

Consider the core principles you want to impart to your children and how you actively work towards nurturing those qualities within them.

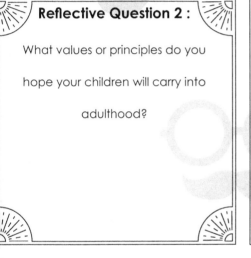

Reflective Question 2 :

What values or principles do you hope your children will carry into adulthood?

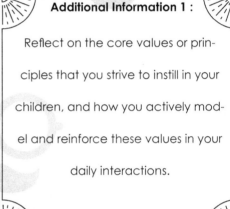

Additional Information 1 :

Reflect on the core values or principles that you strive to instill in your children, and how you actively model and reinforce these values in your daily interactions.

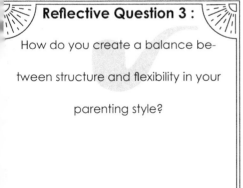

Reflective Question 3 :

How do you create a balance between structure and flexibility in your parenting style?

Additional Information 1 :

Reflect on your approach to establishing routines, rules, and boundaries while allowing space for spontaneity, adaptability, and the individual needs of your children.

Reflective Question 1 :

How do you create special moments and memories with your children?

Additional Information 1 :

Reflect on the ways you prioritize quality time, create traditions, or engage in activities that foster a strong bond and create lasting memories.

Reflective Question 2 :

How do you navigate the challenges of technology and screen time in your children's lives?

Additional Information 1 :

Explore your strategies for managing technology use and screen time in a balanced and responsible way, considering the potential impact on your children's development and well-being.

Reflective Question 3 :

How do you foster a growth mindset in your children and encourage them to embrace challenges and learn from failures?

Additional Information 1 :

Explore your strategies for promoting a positive mindset, resilience, and a willingness to learn and grow in the face of challenges or setbacks.

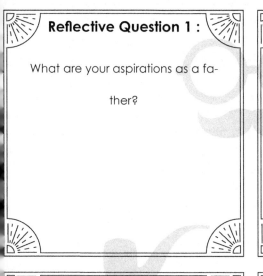

Reflective Question 1 :

What are your aspirations as a father?

Additional Information 1 :

Think about the kind of relationship you want to have with your children as they grow older and the dreams and hopes you hold for their future.

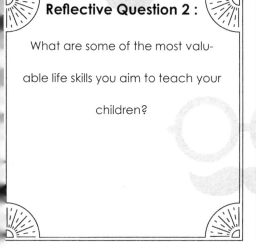

Reflective Question 2 :

What are some of the most valuable life skills you aim to teach your children?

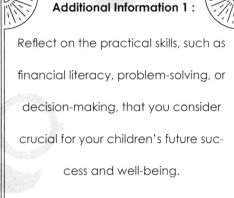

Additional Information 1 :

Reflect on the practical skills, such as financial literacy, problem-solving, or decision-making, that you consider crucial for your children's future success and well-being.

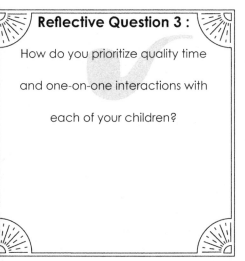

Reflective Question 3 :

How do you prioritize quality time and one-on-one interactions with each of your children?

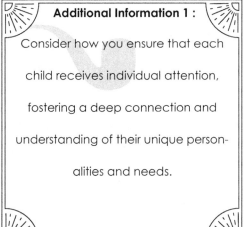

Additional Information 1 :

Consider how you ensure that each child receives individual attention, fostering a deep connection and understanding of their unique personalities and needs.

Dad's Own Jokes

Calling all dads with a knack for humor! In this section, we invite you, dear dad, to unleash your creativity and wit by writing your own jokes. Show off your unique sense of humor and entertain your loved ones with personalized jokes that reflect your style and experiences. Whether you prefer puns, one-liners, or clever wordplay, this is your chance to shine as the resident jokester. Get ready to tickle funny bones and elicit laughter with your own brand of humor. Remember, the best jokes come from the heart and bring joy to those around you. So, grab a pen, let your imagination run wild, and let the laughter begin!

Printed in Great Britain
by Amazon

23813304R00071